TEST PILOT

BY JOHN HAMILTON

BF-03

A&D Xtreme
An imprint of Abdo Publishing | www.abdopublishing.com

Visit us at
www.abdopublishing.com

 PRINTED ON RECYCLED PAPER

Editor: Sue Hamilton
Graphic Design: Sue Hamilton
Cover Design: Sue Hamilton
Cover Photo: U.S. Air Force-Senior Airman Maeson L. Elleman
Interior Photos: AP-pgs 10-11, 17 & 30-31; Corbis-pgs 8-9; Glow Images-pgs 2-3; Library of Congress-pgs 14-15 & 16; Lockheed Martin-1 & 32; NASA-pgs 12, 20 & 21; National Test Pilot School-pg 27; Science Source-pg 13; U.S. Air Force-pgs 4-5, 6-7, 18-19, 22-23, 24-25, 26 (top) & 28-29; U.S. Navy-pg 26 (bottom).

Websites
To learn more
about Xtreme Jobs, visit
booklinks.abdopublishing.com. These
links are routinely monitored and updated to
provide the most current information available.

Library of Congress Control Number: 2015930954

Cataloging-in-Publication Data

Hamilton, John.
 Test pilot / John Hamilton.
  p. cm. -- (Xtreme jobs)
 ISBN 978-1-62403-761-0
 1. Test pilots--Juvenile literature.   I. Title.
 629.130--dc23

                                                2015930954

CONTENTS

Pushing the Edge 4

Experimental Test Pilots 8

Production Test Pilots 10

Astronaut Test Pilots 12

The Wright Brothers 14

Charles Lindbergh 16

Chuck Yeager 18

Neil Armstrong 20

Education 22

Test Pilot School 24

Job Facts 28

Glossary 30

Index 32

PUSHING THE EDGE

An advanced fighter jet loaded with bombs loses control. It begins tumbling out of the sky. For most pilots, it is a nightmare situation. For test pilots, it is just another day on the job.

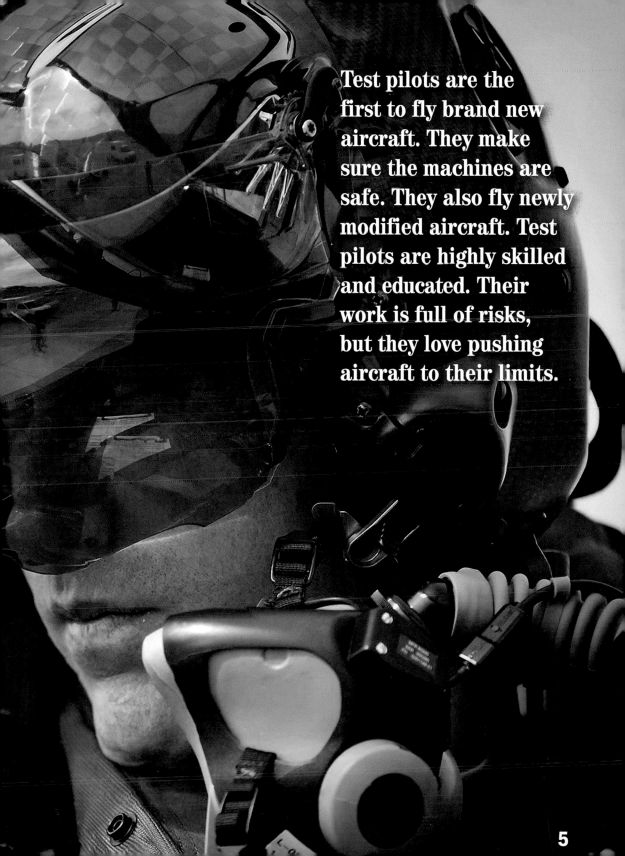

Test pilots are the first to fly brand new aircraft. They make sure the machines are safe. They also fly newly modified aircraft. Test pilots are highly skilled and educated. Their work is full of risks, but they love pushing aircraft to their limits.

Test pilots have thousands of hours of flight experience. They are also well educated. More than half of their job is spent on the ground planning each flight. While flying, they collect scientific data. Then they report back to the aircraft designers.

Flying new aircraft can be very dangerous. There are many unknown risks. Malfunctions can cause aircraft to fly poorly or crash. Test pilots coolly deal with such risks. They make sure the pilots who come after them can depend on the safety of their aircraft.

XTREME FACT – Test pilots face danger every day, but gone are the days when they "kick the tires and light the fires." Today's test pilots plan well in advance to make their job as safe as possible.

EXPERIMENTAL TEST PILOTS

Experimental test pilots fly planes that have never been flown before. Many are military aircraft. Experimental test pilots also check new aircraft modifications. These might include advanced navigation or weapons systems.

Experimental test pilots work closely with engineers and aircraft designers. During flight, they take notes and collect information. They also deal with accidents or malfunctions. Back on the ground, they help analyze data and suggest modifications to make aircraft fly safely.

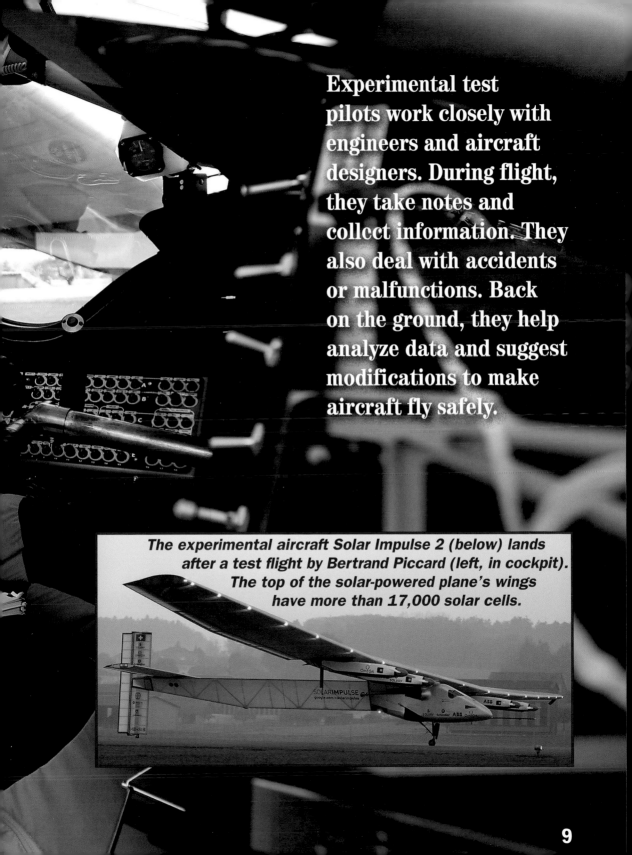

The experimental aircraft Solar Impulse 2 (below) lands after a test flight by Bertrand Piccard (left, in cockpit). The top of the solar-powered plane's wings have more than 17,000 solar cells.

PRODUCTION TEST PILOTS

Production test pilots work for airplane companies such as Boeing or Lockheed Martin. These aviators make sure all new airplanes that come off the assembly line fly the way they are designed to, even during emergencies.

A chase plane (above) follows the test flight of a Boeing 787 Dreamliner aircraft.

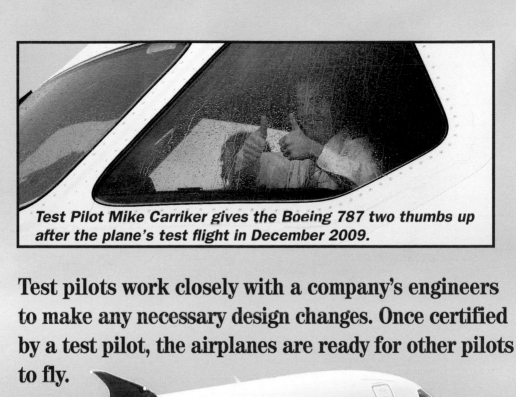

Test Pilot Mike Carriker gives the Boeing 787 two thumbs up after the plane's test flight in December 2009.

Test pilots work closely with a company's engineers to make any necessary design changes. Once certified by a test pilot, the airplanes are ready for other pilots to fly.

ASTRONAUT TEST PILOTS

Most astronauts of the 1960s and 1970s were test pilots. The National Aeronautics and Space Administration (NASA) wanted people who could handle the risks of being in space. Test pilots worked with engineers to design spaceships, including the space shuttle.

NASA test pilots stand in front of the space shuttle prototype Enterprise, *which sits on the 747 Shuttle Carrier Aircraft.*

Fitz Fulton   **Gordon Fullerton**   **Vic Horton**   **Fred Haise**   **Vincent Alvarez**   **Tom McMurtry**

Artwork showing a space tourism ship.

Today, private companies are building spacecraft. They include Virgin Galactic, XCOR Aerospace, SpaceX, Orbital Sciences, and others. They will deliver scientists and supplies to the International Space Station (ISS). They also plan to build spaceships that can be used for space tourism, to launch satellites, and to travel to Mars and beyond. These companies hire test pilots to help them design and fly the spaceships of the future.

THE WRIGHT BROTHERS

Orville Wright   Wilbur Wright

American brothers Orville and Wilbur Wright were the first aviators to build and fly a heavier-than-air, self-powered aircraft. In 1903, they launched their Wright Flyer I at Kitty Hawk, North Carolina.

Like modern test pilots, the Wright brothers studied the science of flight. They experimented and collected data. They never gave up. They learned from their mistakes. After years of trial and error, they created a flying machine that changed the world forever.

The first flight of the Wright Flyer I on December 17, 1903. Orville is piloting. Wilbur runs at the wingtip.

XTREME QUOTE – "If birds can glide for long periods of time, then why can't I?"
–Orville Wright

CHARLES LINDBERGH

In 1927, American Charles Lindbergh became the first person to fly a nonstop solo trip across the Atlantic Ocean. His plane was called *Spirit of St. Louis*. He flew from New York City to Paris, France, in 33 hours, 30 minutes.

Before "Lucky Lindy" made his historic flight, he studied engineering. He flew dangerous missions as a U.S. Army aviator. He was also an airmail carrier. Lindbergh teamed up with Ryan Airlines of San Diego, California. They built a brand-new plane. Lindbergh's flight tests helped the engineers at Ryan modify it. These changes made *Spirit of St. Louis* safe enough for Lindbergh to fly into the history books.

A huge crowd surrounds Lindbergh's Spirit of St. Louis *plane* in Paris in 1927.

CHUCK YEAGER

Charles "Chuck" Yeager was a U.S. Air Force test pilot at a time when jet aircraft were first being flown. In 1947, he became the first person to fly faster than the speed of sound (about 700 miles per hour (1,127 km/hr) at 43,000 feet (13,106 m)). Yeager flew dozens of combat missions during World War II. He became a test pilot after the war. New jet aircraft often crashed. Yeager stayed focussed even during extreme stress.

After breaking the sound barrier with the Bell X-1, Yeager flight tested many kinds of new jet aircraft. He rose to the rank of brigadier general. Yeager was definitely a test pilot who had "the right stuff."

XTREME FACT – Yeager named his Bell X-1 *Glamorous Glennis, after his wife.*

NEIL ARMSTRONG

Before astronaut Neil Armstrong commanded the 1969 Apollo 11 Moon-landing mission, he was a test pilot. He worked for the government agency that later became the National Aeronautics and Space Administration (NASA).

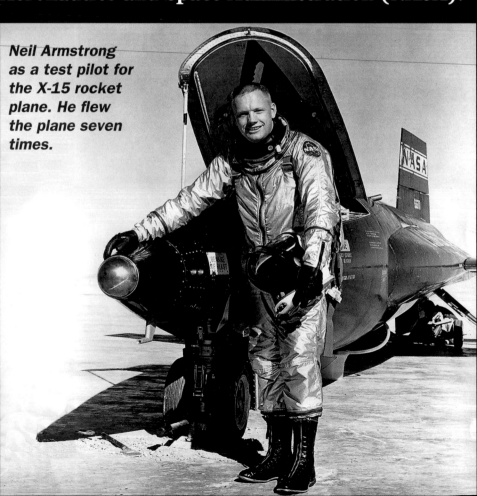

Neil Armstrong as a test pilot for the X-15 rocket plane. He flew the plane seven times.

As an astronaut, Armstrong's quick thinking and expert piloting skills saved two space missions. In 1966, Armstrong's Gemini 8 spaceship began spinning dangerously fast. Armstrong regained control and landed safely. During the Apollo 11 Moon landing, the *Eagle* lunar module's computer almost crashed the craft into a field of boulders. Armstrong's test piloting skills took over. He used manual control to land safely. A short time later, he became the first man to walk on the Moon.

Neil Armstrong makes final prelaunch checks in the Gemini 8 spaceship.

EDUCATION

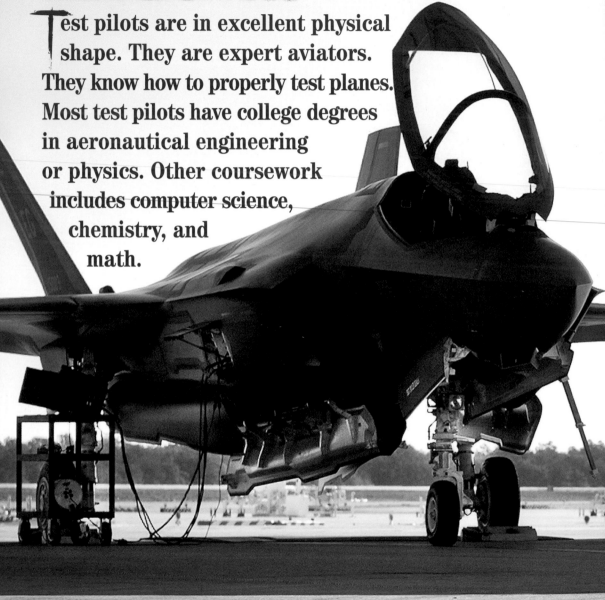

Test pilots are in excellent physical shape. They are expert aviators. They know how to properly test planes. Most test pilots have college degrees in aeronautical engineering or physics. Other coursework includes computer science, chemistry, and math.

Most people get their flight training and education through military experience. The majority of test pilots serve as U.S. Air Force or Navy aviators.

A pilot with the Test and Evaluation Squadron walks toward an F-35A Lightning II to begin flying the new plane.

TEST PILOT SCHOOL

After getting a college degree and learning to fly, test pilots attend a special year-long school. They train in many kinds of aircraft. They learn how to fly safely even when aircraft malfunction. They also learn how to work with aircraft designers, collect data, and write reports. They get hands-on experience with various weapons systems.

RESCUE

0481

A pilot prepares to take off on a training mission in an F-16 Fighting Falcon aircraft.

The U.S. Air Force runs the USAF Test Pilot School at Edwards Air Force Base in California. The school started in 1944, at the dawn of the jet age.

U.S. Navy aviators attend the United States Naval Test Pilot School. It is located at Maryland's Naval Air Station Patuxent River. The Navy also trains pilots from the U.S. Army and Marine Corps. Aviators from other countries also train here.

The National Test Pilot School is located in Mojave, California. It is open to civilian pilots who may not have military flight experience. Many graduates go on to work for aerospace companies such as Sikorsky Aircraft Corp. Many foreign air forces also send pilots to the school for training.

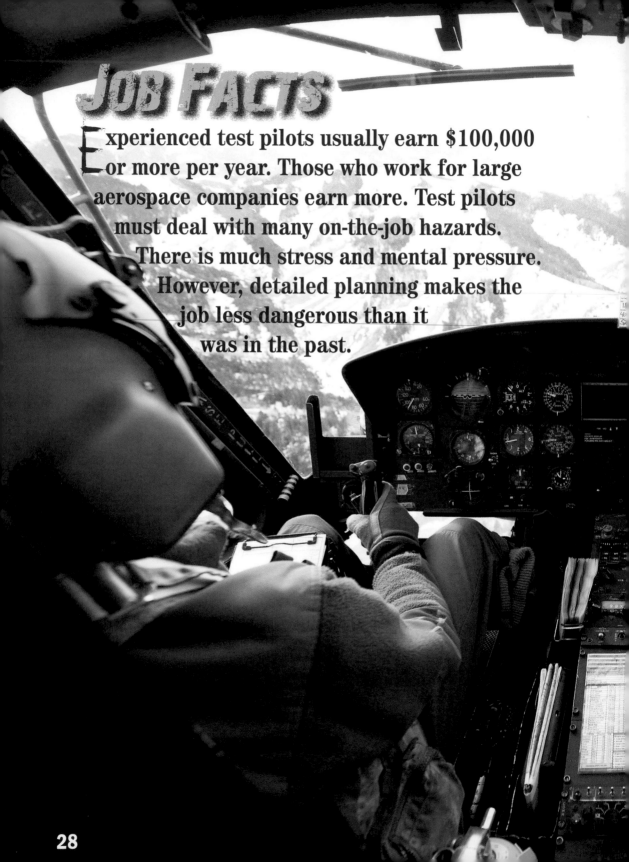

JOB FACTS

Experienced test pilots usually earn $100,000 or more per year. Those who work for large aerospace companies earn more. Test pilots must deal with many on-the-job hazards. There is much stress and mental pressure. However, detailed planning makes the job less dangerous than it was in the past.

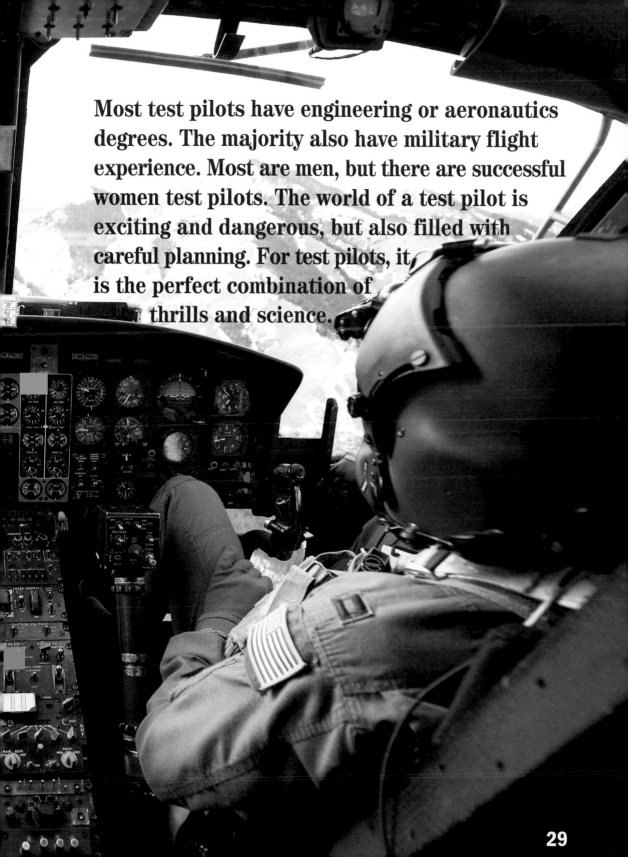

Most test pilots have engineering or aeronautics degrees. The majority also have military flight experience. Most are men, but there are successful women test pilots. The world of a test pilot is exciting and dangerous, but also filled with careful planning. For test pilots, it is the perfect combination of thrills and science.

GLOSSARY

AERONAUTICAL ENGINEERING
An area of study where people design, build, test, or maintain machines that fly. This includes planes, helicopters, rockets, and weapons such as missiles.

APOLLO SPACE PROGRAM
An American space exploration program that ran from 1963 to 1972. Run by NASA, the program's goal was to land astronauts on the Moon and return them safely to Earth. The first Moon landing was achieved by Apollo 11 on July 20, 1969.

INTERNATIONAL SPACE STATION (ISS)
An Earth-orbiting space station designed by NASA, the European Space Agency, the Russian Federal Space Agency, the Japan Aerospace Exploration Agency, and the Canadian Space Agency, as well as other countries around the world. The ISS allows astronauts and scientists to live and work in space. Construction of the ISS began in orbit in 1998.

MALFUNCTION
When a machine or piece of equipment does not operate as it is designed to work. A breakdown.

NATIONAL AERONAUTICS AND SPACE ADMINISTRATION (NASA)
A U.S. government agency started in 1958. NASA's goals include space exploration, as well as increasing people's understanding of Earth, our solar system, and the universe.

Navigation

To provide directions and locations, usually using a computer and satellite system.

Physics

A science that studies the physical properties of something. This includes what it is made of (matter) and the energy it gives off or produces.

The Right Stuff

A person who has the needed combination of intelligence, bravery, and physical traits to do a dangerous or complex job. The phrase became popular after author Tom Wolfe used it as the title of his 1979 book about the first American astronauts selected for the NASA program.

World War II

A war that was fought from 1939 to 1945, involving countries around the world. The United States entered the war after Japan's bombing of the American naval base at Pearl Harbor, in Oahu, Hawaii, on December 7, 1941.

INDEX

A
Air Force, U.S. 4, 18, 23, 26
Alvarez, Vincent 12
Apollo 11 20, 21
Armstrong, Neil 20, 21
Army, U.S. 17, 26
Atlantic Ocean 16

B
Bell X-1 19
Boeing 787 Dreamliner 10, 11
Boeing Company 10

C
California 17, 26, 27
Carriker, Mike 11

D
Dreamliner 10

E
Eagle lunar module 21
Edwards Air Force Base 26
Enterprise 12

F
F-16 Fighting Falcon 25
F-35A Lightning II 23
Fontaine, Troy 4
France 16
Fullerton, Gordon 12
Fulton, Fitz 12

G
Gemini 8 21
Glamorous Glennis 19

H
Haise, Fred 12
Horton, Vic 12

I
International Space Station (ISS) 13

K
Kitty Hawk, NC 14

L
Lindbergh, Charles 16, 17
Lockheed Martin 10
Lucky Lindy 17

M
Marine Corps, U.S. 26
Mars 13
Maryland 26
McMurtry, Tom 12
Mojave, CA 27
Moon 20, 21

N
National Aeronautics and Space Administration (NASA) 12, 20
National Test Pilot School 27
Naval Air Station Patuxent River 26
Navy, U.S. 23, 26
New York City, NY 16
North Carolina 14

O
Orbital Sciences 13

P
Paris, France 16, 17
Piccard, Bertrand 8, 9

R
Ryan Airlines 17

S
747 Shuttle Carrier Aircraft 12
San Diego, CA 17
Sikorsky Aircraft Corp 27
Solar Impulse 2 8, 9
space shuttle 12
SpaceX 13
Spirit of St. Louis 16, 17

T
Test and Evaluation Squadron 23
Test Pilot School, U.S. Air Force 26
Test Pilot School, U.S. Naval 26
"the right stuff" 19

V
Virgin Galactic 13

W
World War II 18
Wright, Orville 14, 15
Wright, Wilbur 14, 15
Wright Flyer I 14, 15

X
X-15 rocket plane 20
XCOR Aerospace 13

Y
Yeager, Charles "Chuck" 18, 19